ON FOOT & FINGER

CLIMBING & WALKING CARTOONS

by

Jim Watson

© Jim Watson 1989
ISBN 0902 363 81 6
First published 1986,
Reprinted 1987, 1991

Published by
Cicerone Press
Police Square, Milnthorpe, Cumbria

INTRODUCTION...

Clinging to a lofty slab of rock and suddenly finding one arm is 2 inches shorter than it was at ground level, or squelching through stair-rod rain, who knows where, blistered and marooned in your £2 trainers, isn't usually a lot of laughs.

Not until later, that is.

A day in the outdoors is invariably followed by an evening of reminiscences, drink in hand, with fellow enthusiasts. Convivial comedians to a man. Or woman. Or, usually, to anybody who will listen. The events of the day are reported, suitably jazzed up for maximum amusement.

I haven't experienced all the situations depicted in this book - thank - goodness - but I'd like to share them with you anyway.

Suitably jazzed up, of course!

I hope you find something familiar in the cartoons. Look-out though - it might be yourself!

So let's reminisce and, ..er ..get the drinks in!

Jim Watson

RUGBY. 1986.

TODAY, WE'RE GOING TO RESCUE SKIDDAW
MOUNTAIN RESCUE
Jim Watson

THESE BINOCULARS BRING EVERYTHING CLOSER AND CLOSER!

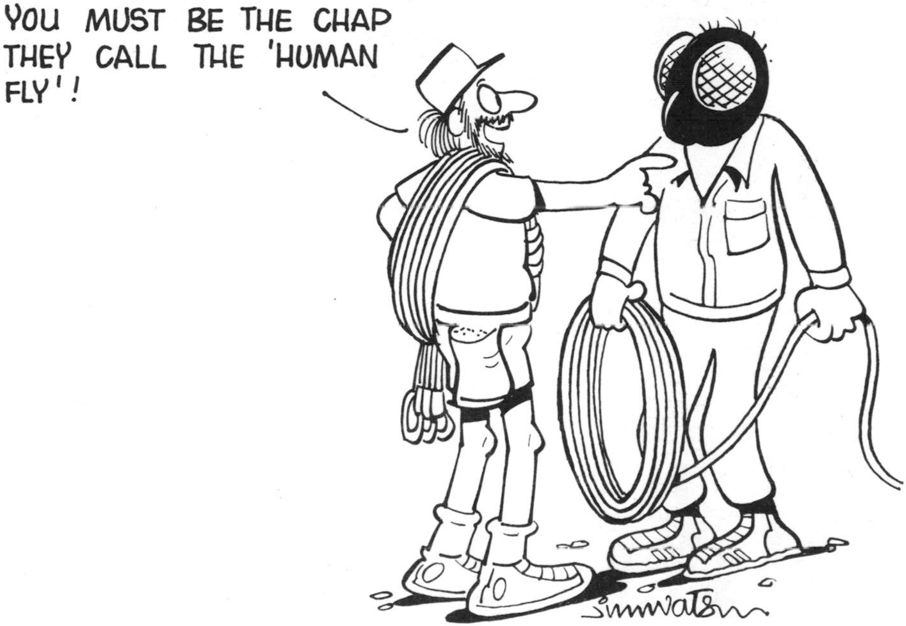
YOU MUST BE THE CHAP THEY CALL THE 'HUMAN FLY'!
jimwatson

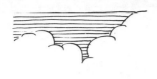

DO YOU HAVE TO TRY OUT **EVERYTHING**?
GUARANTEED WATERPROOF
JimWatson

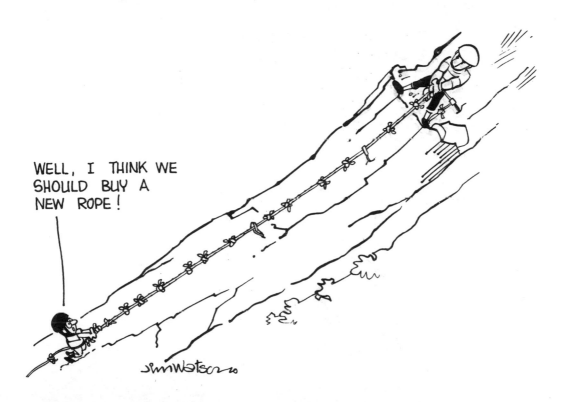

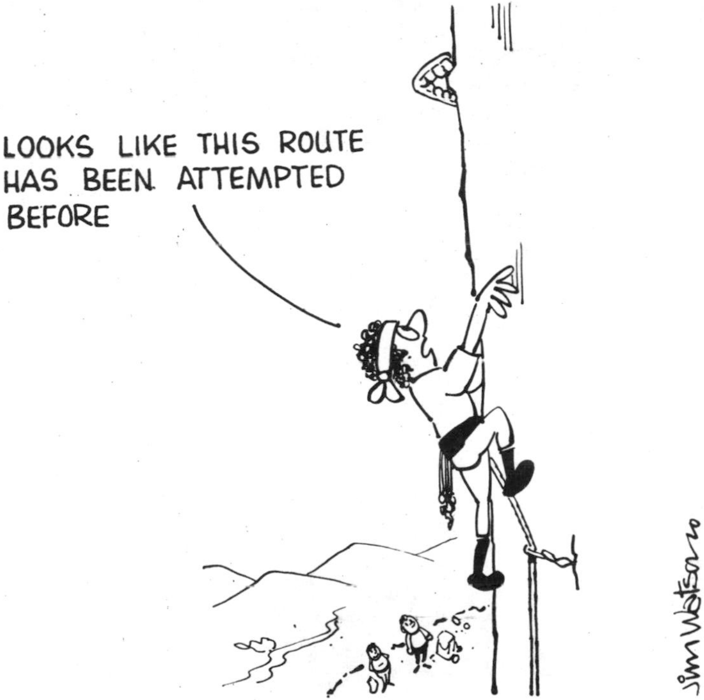
LOOKS LIKE THIS ROUTE HAS BEEN ATTEMPTED BEFORE
Jim Watson

YOU SURE YOU DIDN'T BRING THAT ANTI-MIDGE CREAM?

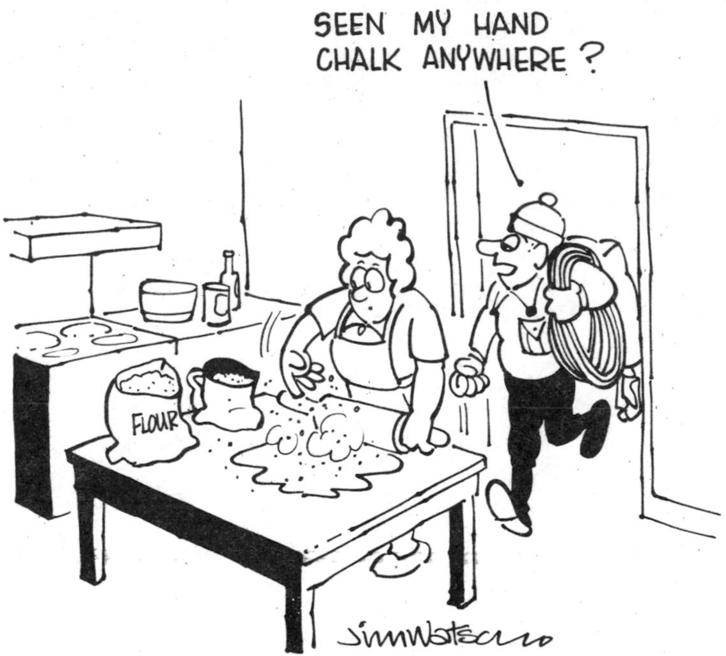
SEEN MY HAND CHALK ANYWHERE ?
FLOUR
JimWatson

PRINTED BY
CARNMOR PRINT & DESIGN, LONDON ROAD, PRESTON.

for
ANYTHING
drawn....
JIM WATSON
25 FROBISHER RD
RUGBY. CV22 7HU.